Marian Cox

Cambridge Checkpoint
English
Workbook
8

CAMBRIDGE
UNIVERSITY PRESS

University Printing House, Cambridge CB2 8BS, United Kingdom

One Liberty Plaza, 20th Floor, New York, NY 10006, USA

477 Williamstown Road, Port Melbourne, VIC 3207, Australia

4843/24, 2nd Floor, Ansari Road, Daryaganj, Delhi – 110002, India

79 Anson Road, #06–04/06, Singapore 079906

Cambridge University Press is part of the University of Cambridge.

It furthers the University's mission by disseminating knowledge in the pursuit of education, learning and research at the highest international levels of excellence.

www.cambridge.org
Information on this title: www.cambridge.org/9781107663152

© Cambridge University Press 2013

This publication is in copyright. Subject to statutory exception
and to the provisions of relevant collective licensing agreements,
no reproduction of any part may take place without the written
permission of Cambridge University Press.

First published 2013

20 19 18 17 16 15

Printed in Dubai by Oriental Press

A catalogue record for this publication is available from the British Library

ISBN 978-1-107-66315-2 Paperback

Cambridge University Press has no responsibility for the persistence or accuracy of URLs for external or third-party internet websites referred to in this publication, and does not guarantee that any content on such websites is, or will remain, accurate or appropriate.

Contents

Introduction v

Unit 1 Fire 1
sequencing notes for particular purposes; difficult spellings; irregular verb forms; past simple, present perfect and past perfect tenses; complex connectives; using 'would' for repeated action in the past; metaphors and similes

Unit 2 Games and sports 10
modal verbs; passives; noun endings; parentheses; relative clauses; complex sentences; sequencing and editing information; varying vocabulary

Unit 3 Water 18
structuring and paraphrasing; present and past participles; prefixes; semi-colons; collective nouns; comparative amounts

Unit 4 The feast 25
adjectival endings; time adverbs and adverbial phrases; the present simple tense for verbs of perception; writing descriptive phrases; iambic pentameter and sonnet form

Unit 5 Other lives 32
linking sentences; forming sentences; writing factual description; prefixes; using imagery; using 'affect' and 'effect'; identifying descriptive devices; writing formal letters

Unit 6 The race 40
viewpoint; prepositions; sentence structures; past participles; semi-colons; difficult spellings

Unit 7 Time and history 45
prefixes; positioning of 'only'; dashes; sentence structures; pronouns of amount; writing news headlines; reading a timetable

Unit 8 Exotic places 52
writing imaginative and factual descriptions; sequencing material; complex sentence formation; colons and semi-colons; speech introduction words; similes and metaphors

Unit 9 Travel and transport 59
using adjectives and intensifiers for description; connotations and evocation

Unit 10 Animal behaviour 67
building vocabulary; evaluating synonyms; paraphrasing; using emphatic adverbials; selecting, sequencing and connecting material

Unit 11 Music and dance 75
figurative language; negative phrasing and understatement for emphasis; using tenses with time adverbials; passive form; hyphens; commas; colloquial and idiomatic English; 'continual' and 'continuous'

Unit 12 A load of nonsense 82
homographs and pronunciation and spelling anomalies; commas in defining and non-defining relative clauses; reported speech; forms of the future tense; colons and semi-colons; speech punctuation; description of process and place

Acknowledgements 90

Introduction

Welcome to Cambridge Checkpoint English Stage 8.

The Cambridge Checkpoint English course covers the Cambridge Secondary 1 English framework and is divided into three stages: 7, 8 and 9.

This Workbook has 12 units which offer support in the skills covered in the corresponding units of the Stage 8 Coursebook. The topics in the Workbook are linked to the topics in the Coursebook. This Workbook is mainly based on descriptive and informative reading and writing.

There are two more workbooks in the series to cover stages 7 and 9, and these provide practice for progressive skills to match the skills covered in the corresponding coursebooks.

The Workbook exercises give extra practice in specific areas for students working alone or for students who need to develop a particular and relevant language skill or task approach.

The rules and key points introduced in the Coursebook are reinforced in the corresponding units of the Workbook, to make sure they have been fully understood and applied before students progress to the next unit.

The Workbook can be used as a differentiation resource for classroom work and for setting homework. The responses can be written in the spaces beneath the exercises. The introduction to each unit tells you the types of exercise it includes.

The answers to the Workbook exercises are on the Teacher Resource CD, which contains further relevant tasks, worksheets and handouts to support each of the Coursebook and Workbook units.

UNIT 1 Fire

This unit gives you practice in sequencing notes for particular purposes; difficult spellings; using irregular verb forms and past simple, present perfect and past perfect tenses; using complex connectives; using 'would' for repeated action in the past; metaphors and similes.

1 Read the notes below and on page 2, which give factual information about the eruption of a volcano in Chile in 2011.

a Put the facts in an appropriate order for a news report, published the day after the eruption, by numbering them.

Volcanic eruption in Chile

- Eruption in the Puyehue-Cordon Caulle volcanic chain approximately 800 km south of capital, Santiago

- Border crossing into Argentina closed

- Ash cover and weather conditions – difficult to see which of the chain's four volcanoes had erupted

- Constant seismic activity and smell of sulphur

Cambridge Checkpoint English 8

- 10-kilometre-high gas column from explosion

- Government evacuating 3500 people from the area

- Huge flames and lightning flashes

- Wind blew ash to Argentina, making the sky dark and grey. Rivers swollen

- Airports in Argentina forced to close flights likely to remain suspended until middle of next week

- Authorities in southern Chile and Argentina monitoring direction of ash clouds

- A change of wind direction sent ash back to the Chilean side

- Public activities in Argentina cancelled

- Chilean health ministry has distributed face masks and eye drops to residents in the area

- Many residents left but some stayed with their homes and animals

- The mayor of Lago Ranco, a town about 70 km north of the volcano range, said that the situation was complex and unpredictable because of the way in which the wind was shifting direction

- There has not been a major eruption of the volcano chain since a huge earthquake in 1960

- Chile is one of the most volcanic countries on Earth. Along its length are around 3000 volcanoes – 80 of them active

b Transfer your notes into the lines on the next page:
- expanding them into sentences
- joining the information logically
- changing them into your own words where possible
- removing repetition
- using short, simple words and sentences.

Leave the first line blank so that you can write your headline when you have finished your report.

UNIT 1 Fire

c Write a suitable headline at the top of your report. Think of a subheading and write it in the margin next to where you would put it in your report.

Cambridge Checkpoint English 8

2 **Look at the information below.**

> forest fire outside Capetown – started by piece of glass left by family having a picnic – ground very dry – no fatalities – strong wind – temperatures high for several days – holiday homes nearby – people had enough time to escape – occurred last month – fire brigade not able to contain the fire – seaplanes dropped water from the sea – large area of forest destroyed – took two days to extinguish flames

a Decide on the most logical order for the information to be used in a witness account, and put numbers above each note to show the sequence.

b Now turn the numbered notes into a paragraph of continuous writing, using participle phrases and a range of connectives to form complex sentences.

UNIT 1 Fire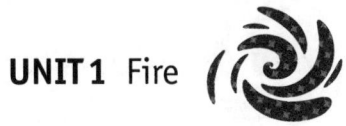

3 The words in bold in the sentences below are often confused or misspelt.

a Circle the correct word in each pair. Learn the differences between them by looking up their meaning in a dictionary if you don't already know it.

  i Their attention was caught by the **fiery/firey** glow from the top of the mountain.

  ii The shop at the corner of the street sells newspapers and **stationary/stationery**.

  iii We recognised the actor who **starred/stared** in the soap opera we watched every evening.

  iv If you **proceed/precede** to the information desk you will be told how to find the main exhibition hall.

  v If you want to **lay/lie** down, you can use the spare bedroom. Your luggage is **laying/lying** in the hall. You can **lay/lie** your coat on the sofa for now and hang it up later.

  vi He **wandered/wondered** through the woods, **wandering/wondering** where exactly he was.

  vii The **affect/effect** of the words was powerful, and the audience was so **affected/effected** that many people burst into tears.

  viii A **complimentary/complementary** ticket was sent to each member of the club.

  ix The **principal/principle** reason for doing it was that it was a matter of **principal/principle**.

  x When they saw the man with the **scared/scarred** face they felt very **scared/scarred**.

b Think of mnemonics (ways of remembering them) so that you know the right spellings in future, e.g. c*ar*s are station*ar*y (both contain *ar*) but pap*er* is station*er*y (both contain *er*).

4 Replace each of the verb plus adverb phrases below with a single verb which would mean the same thing. You may need a thesaurus to help you. There may be more than one possible answer. Then write a sentence containing the verb you have selected.

a run fast ....

....

b look closely ....

....

c complain lengthily ....

....

d tear violently ....

....

e think deeply ....

....

f want desperately ....

....

g walk unsteadily ....

....

5 **Fill in the blank spaces in the table of irregular verb forms below.**

Present	Past	Past participle
drive	drove	
sink		sunk
cut	cut	
lose		lost
take		taken
ride	rode	
think	thought	
sell		sold
know	knew	
lay		laid

UNIT 1 Fire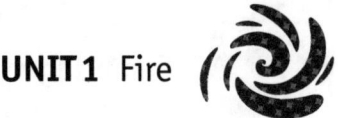

6 Put the verbs into the correct tense in the sentences below: past simple, present perfect or past perfect. There is more than one possibility in some cases.

a They .... (rise) at dawn and since then they .... (have) nothing to eat.

b When I first .... (see) the cloud appear in the sky, I .... (shake) in fear. Since then, I .... (feel) increasingly alarmed.

c The plates still .... (lie) on the table, but someone .... (break) one of them.

d They finally .... (find) the treasure which they .... (seek) for ten years.

e Since leaving school, my elder brother .... (not be able) to find a suitable job, but during the summer holidays he .... (work) for a week as a waiter.

7 Give the present and past participles of the following verbs (e.g. *give* → *giving* → *given*).

a do ....   f feel ....

b go ....   g fall ....

c hear ....   h run ....

d say ....   i pay ....

e leave ....   j lie ....

8 Fill the gaps in these sentences with an appropriate connective. Do not use any connective more than once.

.... I realised that the fire alarm was for real, I set off towards the fire exit. Previously, ... the alarm had sounded, we had not been worried .... we knew it was just a drill. .... I was leaving the building, I could hear shouting. There was no sign of the sales staff, ... worked on the top floor. I realised that the lift was not working, and that .... the stairs to the upper floors were cut off by the fire, the people there would be in danger, ... someone rescued them. .... I am not normally a quick-thinking person, I ran over to the firefighters, ... they had arrived on the scene, to tell them that I thought there were people trapped inside the building. I pointed to the top floor, ... now had flames leaping out of it.

9 Some of the verbs in the sentences below could be changed to the 'would' plus verb form to show a repeated action in the past. Put a tick or a cross next to each verb to signify whether the 'would' form is appropriate.

a Each year, in the autumn, they *collect* [ ] enough firewood to last through the winter.

b Last January I *go* [ ] skiing and came back with my leg in plaster.

c She *watch* [ ] the quiz programme on Monday evening and *shout* [ ] out the answers.

d Every time the postman *try* [ ] to deliver a parcel, the dog *throw* [ ] itself at the door in a frenzy.

e As I hadn't received any information about the job, I *decide* [ ] not to attend the interview, which *take* [ ] place the following day.

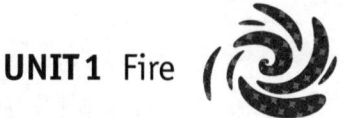

UNIT 1 Fire

10 Overused metaphors or similes become clichés and spoil descriptive writing. Paraphrase the following using specific and interesting words (e.g. *He looked as if his life was an uphill struggle* could become *He looked careworn and despondent*) or your own original comparisons (e.g. *He looked as though tomorrow was his enemy*).

a Her teeth were as white as pearls.

....

b They looked as though butter wouldn't melt in their mouths.

....

c The old man with twinkling blue eyes had been around for donkey's years.

....

d The horse ran like the wind.

....

e The visitors were hogging all the limelight.

....

f My teacher talked until he was blue in the face.

....

g The kittens in the basket looked as pretty as a picture.

....

UNIT 2 Games and sports

This unit looks at modal verbs, passives and noun endings. You will practise constructing and punctuating parentheses, relative clauses and complex sentences; sequencing and editing information; and using varied vocabulary.

1 Use 'whichever', 'whoever', 'whatever', or 'whenever' in the spaces in the sentences below. There may be more than one possible answer.

a We can start at either six or seven o'clock, ... suits you.

b Bring .... you can persuade to come, otherwise there won't be enough people for a team.

c .... are you playing? I've never seen a game like this before.

d You can practise here .... you have some free time.

e .... they were, they demanded the right to do .... they wanted, ... they wanted.

2 Put pairs of brackets and/or dashes in these sentences, in the correct places. Additional commas may also be needed.

a Backgammon or *tavli* is less popular nowadays thanks to the invention of video games but still widely played in many countries particularly those around the Mediterranean.

b There is a difference a huge difference between playing a sport to win and playing to enjoy the match and nowadays too many people are only interested in coming first.

c There are many types of running some short and some long distance so there's no excuse for not keeping fit something which is especially necessary if you sit all day at a desk.

d Different countries have different favourite sports as is apparent during the Olympic Games and this is often because of the climate for example skiing is usually performed best by countries which have a lot of snow.

e Some sports are controversial horse racing for instance because of the danger of permanent physical damage to both human and animal participants.

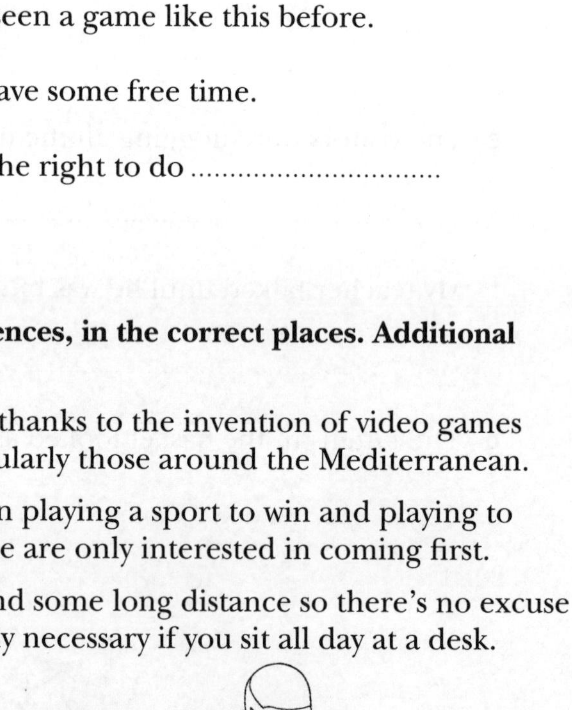

UNIT 2 Games and sports

3 Put commas in the sentences below to indicate the phrases in apposition (phrases which mean the same thing as the previous word or phrase and are not strictly necessary to the sentence).

   a   The captain of the squad Domingo Fernandez was the first to score a goal the first goal of the season.

   b   When the team coach arrived at the border the crossing between Romania and Bulgaria there was a long delay.

   c   I've spoken to Mr Shafiz the head of PE at the other school and he agrees that we should postpone the fixture since so many players boys and girls are off sick at the moment.

   d   Send me a message phone call or email if you change your mind about wanting to be in the swimming team.

   e   The trophy a large gold plate was held up to the camera by the winner of the tennis final the last match of the season.

4 Put 'must', 'should', 'could' or 'would' in the gaps in the passage below.

Horse riding is a popular activity in many parts of the world. There are things you .... know for your safety before you get on a horse. You .... always approach it and lead it around from its left side. You .... not stand immediately behind it or you .... be kicked. It .... be sensible to wear a hat when riding in case of a fall, which .... be fatal.

Another thing which .... be remembered when on horseback is that you .... always be in control of the horse. .... you be feeling nervous, the horse .... be able to tell.

Cambridge Checkpoint English 8

5 Change active verbs to the passive form where possible in the passage below, and rewrite the passage in the lines provided. Some verbs may need to be changed to a synonymous verb which can be used passively.

> Two to four players play the game. First deal seven cards to each player. The player to the left of the dealer starts the game. They lay down their highest card. Players in turn lay down a card, following suit. The player who places the highest card wins the round and collects the pile of cards. If they don't have a card in the same suit, they don't play in that round. Players replace their used cards from the central pile. When the first player is out, because they have no more cards, the players count the number of piles each player has collected.

....

....

....

....

....

....

....

....

....

....

UNIT 2 Games and sports

6 Give words beginning with the prefix 're' that mean the same as the following phrases.

a carry on ....

b make again ....

c think again ....

d make strong ....

e make the way it was ....

7 Replace the word 'nice' with a more specific, appropriate adjective in the ten places where it is used in the passage.

Yesterday evening I had a really [1] **nice** time to celebrate my birthday. I went to a [2] **nice** restaurant with my family and my best friend, who is very [3] **nice**, and we ordered some [4] **nice** dishes from the menu. The atmosphere was [5] **nice**, as there were [6] **nice** pictures on the wall, and [7] **nice** music was playing. Afterwards, we went to a place where they serve [8] **nice** ice cream, and then we watched a [9] **nice** film when we got home, after looking at all my [10] **nice** presents.

1 .... 6 ....

2 .... 7 ....

3 .... 8 ....

4 .... 9 ....

5 .... 10 ....

8 Some of the sentences below need a comma before the relative pronoun ('who' or 'which') and others do not, depending on whether the relative clause is defining or non-defining (whether it is a necessary part of the subject description or not). Add commas where you think they are needed.

a The man who sells balloons isn't in his usual place today.

b They met the champion swimmer who was South African and he explained his goal which was to win three gold medals in the next Olympics.

c The biggest horse which won the previous race was also the only white one.

d We would like to learn how to play the game which was shown on TV.

e I think I know who you are talking about.

9 Underline the words below that are both nouns and also another part of speech. Circle the words which are not nouns at all.

a captive

b safe

c trouble

d deliberate

e patience

f tranquillity

g blazing

h concern

i danger

j extinguish

10 Change these verbs and adjectives into nouns. Some may have more than one possible ending. Take care with spelling when you make the change.

a concentrate ....

b interfere ....

c acquaint ....

d receive ....

e entertain ....

f satisfy ....

g dispose ....

h familiar ....

i kind ....

j wise ....

11 Read the passage below about the invention of chess and then answer the questions.

Have you ever wondered who invented chess?
   When I was about 12 years old my uncle once told me a story about how chess was invented.
   Hundreds and hundreds of years ago there was a King in India who loved to play games. But he had got bored of the games that were present at the time and wanted a new game that was much more challenging. He commissioned a poor mathematician who lived in his kingdom to come up with a new game. After months of struggling with all kinds of ideas the mathematician came up with the game of Chaturanga. The game had two armies each led by a King who commanded the army to defeat the other by capturing the enemy King. It was played on a simple 8×8 square board. The King loved this game so much that he offered to give the poor mathematician anything he wished for. 'I would like one grain of rice for

the first square of the board, two grains for the second, four grains for the third and so on, doubled for each of the 64 squares of the game board,' said the mathematician. 'Is that all?' asked the King. 'Why don't you ask for gold or silver coins instead of rice grains?' 'The rice should be sufficient for me,' replied the mathematician. The King ordered his staff to lay down the grains of rice and soon learned that all the wealth in his kingdom would not be enough to buy the amount of rice needed on the 64th square. In fact the whole kingdom's supply of rice was exhausted before the 30th square was reached. 'You have provided me with such a great game and yet I cannot fulfil your simple wish. You are indeed a genius,' said the King, and offered to make the mathematician his topmost advisor instead.

After hearing that story I was obsessed with wanting to know exactly how many grains of rice would be needed on the 64th square and how much total rice would be needed for all 64 squares. Personal computers were not available then (this is around 1978) and so I set out to find the answer using my dad's calculator. I think the calculator had about ten digits on it; and that was considered top of the line then. Within a minute or two of starting, the calculator hit its limit. But I really wanted to know the answer, so I kept going and did the calculations by hand. After spending most of my Sunday morning doing arithmetic, I finally had the answers:

```
9,223,372,036,854,775,808 on the 64th square and
18,446,744,073,709,551,615 total for the whole board
```

That's about 18 billion billion. So if a bag of rice contained a billion grains, you would need 18 billion such bags. But actually a real bag of rice weighing 50 kilograms has less than 3 million grains.

This story about the King is most likely not true. But it is true that there was an ancient Indian game called Chaturanga and it is believed that modern chess evolved from it. However, some scholars argue that China is the true birthplace of chess. So we may never know the real answer.

From **The Story of How Chess was Invented** *by Omar Syed*

a Put square brackets around the information in the passage which you think is not really necessary, or repeats something said earlier.

b Reorder the remaining information by putting numbers above it.

c Write out the numbered parts in sentences in the new sequence, in the space below.

UNIT 2 Games and sports

d Now write it again in the space below, this time using participle phrases and a range of connectives to reduce the number of sentences.

UNIT 3 Water

This unit gives you practice in structuring and paraphrasing; present and past participles; prefixes; and using semi-colons, collective nouns and comparative amounts.

1 The facts below describe how glaciers are formed. Put them into the right order by numbering them. Then draw a diagram in the box and use the facts, in note form, to label it.

The weight of the glacier puts pressure on the land underneath and makes the valley floors.

The snow builds up over several years because it falls more often than it melts.

The pressure of the new snow, over thousands of years, causes the underlying snow to turn to ice.

The glacier carves out and shifts rock as it moves.

The air is forced out of the ice, so that its colour appears to be blue.

UNIT 3 Water

2 Use past participles to make each pair of sentences below into one sentence. You may wish or need to change the order or grammar. Use commas to divide the main clause from the participle phrase.

a They were disappointed by not being able to picnic by the river. They went home sadly.

....

....

b The rain prevented them from playing cricket. They did gymnastics indoors instead.

....

....

c Snow is enjoyed by the majority of people. A few don't like it.

....

....

d The Aswan High Dam in Egypt was built with Russian help. It stopped the seasonal overflowing of the River Nile.

....

....

e The Venice tide barriers cost millions of dollars. They were installed after massive flooding of the city in 1966.

....

....

....

3 Give the irregular past participle form of the following verbs.

a sleep .... f sink ....

b seek .... g run ....

c lie .... h know ....

d swim .... i sew ....

e become .... j dig ....

4 Using the verb given in brackets, put a present or past participle in the gaps in the sentences below.

a .... (realise) that there was going to be a storm, the fishermen did not go out in their boats that day.

b .... (delay) by the flooded roads, we missed the meeting, ... (arrive) half an hour after it finished.

c The drought is causing crops to dry up in an area also .... (burn) by forest fires, ... (leave) very little greenery.

d .... (sell) to the highest bidder in the auction, the painting of a ship at sea was the most interesting of the things .... (find) in the old mansion.

e He finally made it to the shore, ... (swim) against the current the whole way.

UNIT 3 Water

5 Read the passage below and then answer the questions.

Thor Heyerdahl, 1914–2002, anthropologist

Thor Heyerdahl was propelled to fame by his remarkable crossing of the Pacific Ocean aboard a balsa-wood raft, the Kon-Tiki, in 1947. Against all **prevailing** opinion, Heyerdahl was convinced that **traits** common to Polynesia and South America were the result of prehistoric migration by Peruvian Indians, perhaps around 500 BC. Academic orthodoxy held that the journey of 5000 miles central to the theory was beyond such a primitive people.

Since no publisher would print his thesis, Heyerdahl decided that only a re-creation of such a voyage could give his ideas the necessary credibility. With five friends as crew, he constructed a 20 metre raft with sails, its design based on ancient pictures of Indian ocean-going vessels.

The craft was named Kon-Tiki after the mythical Polynesian hero Tiki, said in oral tradition to have led the ancestors of the islanders there from the east. After 4500 nautical miles the raft grounded itself on the Raroia reef and Heyerdahl waded ashore on Tuamotu Island, the southernmost tip of Polynesia.

In later years he came to **resent** the celebrity that Kon-Tiki had brought him, arguing that it had pigeon-holed him as a **daredevil** explorer rather than as a man of science. The story of his voyage eventually sold more than 30 million copies, although when his manuscript was first offered to American publishers it was rejected, on the grounds that the public would not be interested as nobody had drowned.

He remained **trim** into old age, helped by his daily practice of digging a large hole in his garden with a pick and shovel.

Adapted from The Daily Telegraph

a Paraphrase the following expressions from the passage:

   i propelled to fame ....

   ii Academic orthodoxy held that ....

   iii it had pigeon-holed him ....

b Give synonyms for the five words in bold as they are used in the passage.

   i prevailing ....   **iv** daredevil ....

   ii traits ....   **v** trim ....

   iii resent ....

c What do the following prefixes mean, judging from these words from the passage?

  i pro- (propelled) ....

  ii pre- (prehistoric) ....

  iii con- (construct) ....

d Make three lists of other words beginning with the prefixes in exercise 5c.

....

....

....

....

6 Some of the full stops in the passage below could be changed to semi-colons. Circle those you think would be suitable.

It was a beautiful evening when they decided to walk down to the lake. The moon was full and there was no wind. The group of friends from the camp in the woods intended to have a midnight swim. The lake was shallow at the edges and the water would be reasonably warm. Those who didn't know how to swim would content themselves with paddling and splashing each other. The younger ones seemed to enjoy making each other wet at any opportunity. The camp leader realised that the group had left their tents when she heard voices moving through the trees. She followed them at a distance. Just as they were about to enter the lake, she blew her whistle and told them to go back. She said it was too dangerous to go in the lake in darkness. They could come back the following day to swim.

UNIT 3 Water

7 Rewrite the passage below, replacing the semi-colons with commas and connectives. You can change the order of the clauses if you wish.

> The following day, when they went back to the lake, the weather had turned cold; there was a strong northerly breeze. There were waves on the lake, and the water was freezing; none of them wanted to go in. The camp leader tried to persuade them to have a swim; she didn't really want to go in herself. She led the way into the water; no one followed. She turned round to see where they were; they had all run away. When they got back to camp they lit a fire; they felt cold. They wished they had been allowed to swim the previous evening; it would have been much warmer.

....

....

....

....

....

....

....

....

8 What are the collective nouns for a group of the following? Look up those you don't already know, but make a guess first.

    a ants   ....

    b locusts   ....

    c puppies   ....

    d geese ....

    e acrobats ....

    f experts ....

    g thieves ....

    h bananas ....

    i mountains ....

    j stairs ....

9 Choose the correct word or phrase for each of the gaps in the following sentences. One word is used twice.

a little	few	little	less	fewer
much	more	a few	a lot of	many

    a 'How .... of you are there?' the waiter asked. 'There's room for only .... more.'

    b There are .... snow leopards left living in the wild. .... is being done to save the species.

    c I wish I had .... time. I have so .... to do.

    d Every year .... people attend the annual show. The tickets now cost .... money. If they cost .... , more people would go.

    e There is .... hope that there will be a solution. However, there may be .... improvement in the situation.

UNIT 4 The feast

In this unit you will look at adjectival endings; practise using time adverbs and adverbial phrases, and the present simple tense for verbs of perception; write some descriptive phrases; and practise recognising iambic pentameter and sonnet form.

1 Make the following nouns into adjectives by changing their endings. Some may have more than one possible answer. Use a dictionary to check your answers.

a vision ....

b speciality ....

c respect ....

d child ....

e relation ....

f hope ....

g shame ....

h change ....

i scare ....

j variation ....

k reception ....

l suspect ....

m adore ....

n plenty ....

o decency ....

Cambridge Checkpoint English 8

2 Think of ten adjectives of your own, one for each of the following endings.

ible/able   ive   ary   ant/ent   al   itional/ational   ish   etic   ile   y

a ....   f ....

b ....   g ....

c ....   h ....

d ....   i ....

e ....   j ....

3 Make the following numbers into adjectives (e.g. *six* → *sixth*). Think carefully about the spelling.

a three ....   c eight ....   e twelve ....

b five ....   d nine ....

4 Replace the word 'then' with more specific time adverbs (e.g. *Belatedly*) in the ten places where it is used in the passage. Do not use the same time adverb more than once.

[1] **Then** he fell down a hole in the ground. [2] **Then** he picked himself up from his fall. [3] **Then** he found that he was in a kind of cave. [4] **Then** he could see that it was a store room. [5] **Then** he noticed that there were boxes and tins of food piled all around. [6] **Then** he went closer to investigate them. [7] **Then** he realised that he was hungry. [8] **Then** he chose one of the boxes. [9] **Then** he opened it. [10] **Then** he discovered that it was empty.

1 ....   6 ....

2 ....   7 ....

3 ....   8 ....

4 ....   9 ....

5 ....   10 ....

UNIT 4 The feast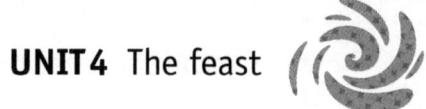

5 Write ten sentences which include the following time adverbs and adverbial phrases, showing their meaning. Think carefully about the verb tense.

| without further ado | after a while | in no time | regularly | finally |
| at the same time | previously | instantly | eventually | during |

a ....

....

b ....

....

c ....

....

d ....

....

e ....

....

f ....

....

g ....

....

h ....

....

i ....

....

j ....

....

6 In the dialogue below, some of the verbs need to be in the present simple because they are verbs of perception, while the others can be in the present continuous. Put each verb in the correct tense.

'I .... (feel) sick. I .... (go) home now.'

'I .... (see) that you haven't finished your meal yet. I .... (think) it would be better to wait until afterwards.'

'I .... (know) that it .... (seem) like a good idea, but it will be worse if I stay longer, and eat more.'

'But the food .... (taste) fine to me, and it .... (look) all right too.'

'I .... (hear) and .... (understand) what you .... (say), but I really .... (believe)

I .... (need) to leave right now.'

7 Study the picture below and then answer the questions on the next page.

UNIT 4 The feast

a List ten items of food and drink that you can identify in the picture.

i .... vi ....

ii .... vii ....

iii .... viii ....

iv .... ix ....

v .... x ....

b Think of a suitable and specific adjective to put in front of each of the items of food and drink you have listed. Think of unusual adjectives that are polysyllabic or have interesting sounds, e.g. *mouth-watering*. Do not use the same adjective twice.

i .... vi ....

ii .... vii ....

iii .... viii ....

iv .... ix ....

v .... x ....

c Join your list of adjectives plus nouns into a piece of continuous descriptive writing about the content of the picnic.

....

....

....

....

....

....

....

Cambridge Checkpoint English 8

....

....

....

....

8 **Tick the lines which are in iambic pentameter.**

a There is no stronger love than love of food.

b I've breakfasted, but now I'd like more toast.

c One cannot sleep and work without food.

d A glass of milk must be a healthy drink.

e Anything is good if made of chocolate.

9 **Complete the lines below with words which fit the metre. First work out how many syllables the word should have, and where the stress should fall.**

a The .... bread is always good to taste.

b I like to watch my .... cook a meal.

c They left with much .... and farewells.

d The quick brown .... stole all the food and fled.

e The sunset colours changed from .... to ....

UNIT 4 The feast

10 The next three questions are on the Shakespeare sonnet below, the lines of which have been jumbled.

   a Give meanings for the following words as they are used in the sonnet. Use a dictionary for words you do not know.

      anon   gluttoning   filching   starved   strife   pine   surfeit   miser

      ....

      ....

      ....

   b Why do you think these words have missing letters replaced by apostrophes?

      sweet-season'd   show'rs   better'd   'twixt

      ....

   c Order the lines of the sonnet correctly by putting a number next to each line. The first two lines are in the right place. The sonnet ends in a couplet and the rest of the lines have an alternate rhyme scheme. The punctuation at the end of each line will help you.

So are you to my thoughts as food to life,	[1]
Or as sweet-season'd show'rs are to the ground;	[2]
Now proud as an enjoyer, and anon	
Or gluttoning on all, or all away.	
Doubting the filching age will steal his treasure;	
Sometime all full with feasting on your sight,	
And by and by clean starved for a look;	
And for the peace of you I hold such strife	
Now counting best to be with you alone,	
Possessing or pursuing no delight	
Then better'd that the world may see my pleasure:	
Save what is had, or must from you be took.	
Thus do I pine and surfeit day by day,	
As 'twixt a miser and his wealth is found.	

UNIT 5 Other lives

This unit gives you practice in linking sentences; forming sentences; writing factual description; using imagery; using 'affect' and 'effect'; using prefixes; identifying descriptive devices; and writing formal letters.

1 Link the sentences below using present participles. For example:

She saw the child. She went towards him. She thought that he was lost.

Seeing the child, she went towards him, thinking that he was lost.

First decide on the best order for the phrases.

a We decided not to go any further. We were afraid of what lived in the woods. We gladly turned back home.

....

....

b I believed I had the right skills. I wanted to earn money during the summer holiday. I applied for the job.

....

....

c The visitors looked intrigued. They used their mobile phones. They took a lot of photographs.

....

....

d The temperature suddenly fell. It became very cold. It made us shiver.

....

....

UNIT 5 Other lives

e The Sahara is the largest tropical desert in the world. The Sahara desert covers 25% of Africa. The Sahara desert fluctuates in size.

....

....

2 Write a description of this American outlaw from the 19th century. Describe his appearance in great detail.

WANTED
$5000 REWARD

Description:

3 Replace the semi-colons in these sentences with different connectives. There are various possible answers. For example:

I have never been to New Zealand; I would like to.

I have never been to New Zealand, though I would like to.

a The purpose of education is to prepare young people for adult life; they need to acquire knowledge and understanding.

b The storm was more severe than the ones they were used to; they were in a mountainous region.

c I don't mind coming with you; I would prefer to stay at home.

d He didn't succeed in getting on the flight to Johannesburg; he tried very hard.

e The trains were delayed; there was snow on the railway line.

UNIT 5 Other lives

4 Imagine that you are looking in the shop window of an expensive jeweller's. Describe some of the jewellery that you can see. Use imagery, and associations, and the sense of touch as well as sight.

....

5 Put the correct form of 'affect' or 'effect' in the gaps in the sentences below. Remember that usually 'affect' is a verb and 'effect' is a noun. 'Effect' can also be a verb, meaning to cause or achieve.

a Her illness .... her badly. She was, in .... , unable to continue her normal life.

b It has a beneficial .... on student performance to make lessons as interesting as possible, as learning is badly .... by boredom.

c They didn't want to .... her chances of success by telling her what the .... on them would be if she got the job.

d We made many attempts to .... the demolition of the unsafe building, as this .... everyone in the neighbourhood.

e He didn't care what the .... would be; he just wanted to leave as quickly as possible; he was, in .... , saying goodbye forever.

6 Fill the ten gaps in the poem with appropriate words. Think about parts of speech, and the sound and rhythm of the poem, before choosing your words.

Baby's world

I wish I could take a .... corner in the heart of my baby's very own world.

I know it has stars that talk to him, and a sky that .... down to his face to amuse him with its .... clouds and rainbows.

Those who make believe to be .... and look as if they never could move, come .... to his window with their stories and with trays crowded with .... toys.

I wish I could travel by the road that .... baby's mind, and out .... all bounds;

Where messengers run errands for no cause between the kingdoms of kings of no history;

Where Reason makes .... of her laws and flies them, the Truth sets Fact free from its ....

Rabindranath Tagore

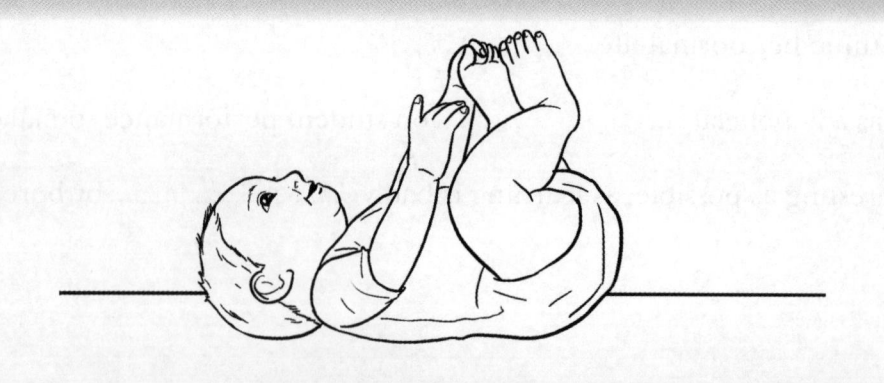

UNIT 5 Other lives

7 Put the correct prefix, 'com'/'con', 'sub'/'sup', or 'sur', on the following word stems. There may be more than one possible answer.

a .... pose

b .... roundings

c .... fortable

d .... tact

e .... test

f .... petitor

g .... prise

h .... face

i .... tract

j .... mit

8 Read the following passage, which has American spelling.

> Everything that could hum, or buzz, or sing, or bloom, had a part in my education – noisy-throated frogs, katydids, and crickets held in my hand until, forgetting their embarrassment, they trilled their reedy note, little downy chickens and wildflowers, the dogwood blossoms, meadow-violets and budding fruit trees. I felt the bursting cotton-bolls and fingered their soft fiber and fuzzy seeds; I felt the low soughing of the wind through the cornstalks, the silky rustling of the long leaves, and the indignant snort of my pony, as we caught him in the pasture and put the bit in his mouth – ah me! how well I remember the spicy, clovery smell of his breath!
>
> Sometimes I rose at dawn and stole into the garden while the heavy dew lay on the grass and flowers. Few know what joy it is to feel the roses pressing softly into the hand, or the beautiful motion of the lilies as they sway in the morning breeze. Sometimes I caught an insect in the

flower I was plucking, and I felt the faint noise of a pair of wings rubbed together in a sudden terror, as the little creature became aware of a pressure from without.

Another favorite haunt of mine was the orchard, where the fruit ripened early in July. The large, downy peaches would reach themselves into my hand, and as the joyous breezes flew about the trees the apples tumbled at my feet. Oh, the delight with which I gathered up the fruit in my pinafore, pressed my face against the smooth cheeks of the apples, still warm from the sun, and skipped back to the house!

From The Story of My Life *by Helen Keller*

a Give examples of monosyllabic words which you think are evocative in the passage.

....

....

b Give examples of present participle forms which you think are effective in the passage.

....

....

c Give examples of each of the senses which have been used in the descriptions in the passage.

....

....

....

d Give examples of the use of assonance, alliteration and consonance (repetition of consonant sounds in close proximity) in the passage.

....

....

....

UNIT 5 Other lives

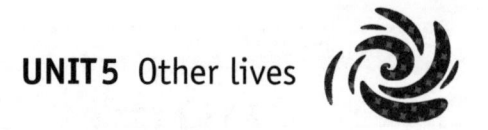

9 Imagine that you want to work in a shop near where you live as a holiday job. Write a formal letter, of three paragraphs, explaining your interest in the job and the skills you possess which would make you a suitable employee.

Dear Sir/Madam

....

....

....

....

....

....

....

....

....

....

....

....

....

....

....

....

....

Yours faithfully

....

UNIT 6 The race

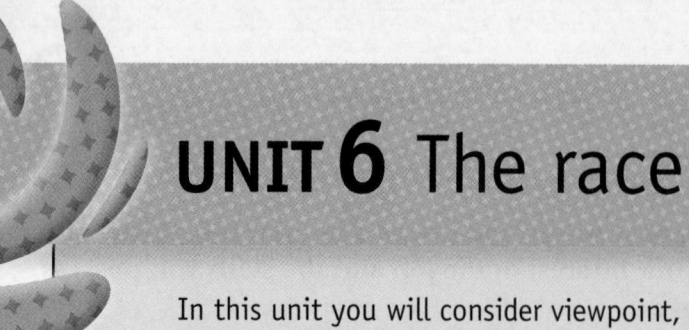

In this unit you will consider viewpoint, and you will also practise prepositions, sentence structures, past participles, semi-colons and difficult spellings.

1 Put the correct prepositions in the 12 gaps below.

The most important aspect .... any kind of racing is attitude. There will always be mistakes made, but you should not dwell .... them. You can consider the mistakes later, and learn .... them, but don't let them interfere with the race .... the time they happen. Do not take offence .... helpful comments; you can always use them .... your advantage .... the future, whatever source they come .... Keep .... mind that all skills need constant practice. Make a list of priorities, ... the goal of making the maximum amount of improvement possible. You will improve most by concentrating .... skills you don't already do particularly well. Make yourself try out tips given to you .... better racers than you.

UNIT 6 The race

2 Write the correct version next to the words which you think are misspelt below. Check your answers in a dictionary, and also look at any meanings you did not know.

a manageing ....
b savage ....
c gauge ....
d leages ....
e gaurantee ....

f gesticulate ....
g regection ....
h disgise ....
i genes ....
j guile ....

3 Write 'apart from' or 'except for' in the gaps in the sentences below.

a There was no one in the stadium, ... one athlete training on the track.

b .... food, the new supermarket sells many things.

c She participated in many other sports .... hockey, tennis and volleyball.

d Everyone, ... Sebastian, thought that Shan had won all the races .... the last one.

e The new champion said nothing, ... thank you and goodbye.

4 Use a variety of ways (connectives, relative pronouns, or past participles) to join each pair of sentences below into one sentence.

a They were defeated in the basketball match. They went home sadly.

....

....

b The game of chess was invented many centuries ago. It isn't certain whether it was first played by the Indians or the Chinese.

....

....

....

c Sport is enjoyed by the majority of people. A few don't like it.

....

....

d Brian Lara was born in 1969. He was a legendary West Indian batsman.

....

....

e The stadium cost millions of dollars to build. It was completed just in time for the Olympic Games.

....

....

5 **Put semi-colons in the correct places in the sentences below.**

    a There were many different kinds of people in the crowd: schoolchildren teenagers in groups tourists locals having a day out.

    b I enjoy the following pastimes: horse riding in the countryside reading comics playing with my pet rabbit swimming emailing my friends and family.

    c There are five stages in making an omelette: prepare the filling beat the eggs pour the mixture in the pan and let it cook put the filling in fold the omelette over and serve it.

    d First, look both ways second, check again third, walk across the road quickly but do not run.

    e She went hopping around the garden she went skipping around the garden she went dancing around the garden.

UNIT 6 The race

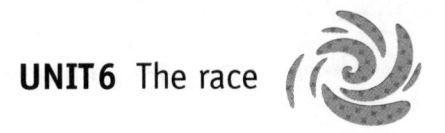

6 Give the past participle of the following verbs. Think about whether you need to double the final 'l' or 't' before adding the suffix.

a commit ....
b profit ....
c repeat ....
d submit ....
e label ....
f revel ....
g target ....
h reveal ....
i pedal ....
j patrol ....

7 Look at the cartoon and write two single-paragraph accounts of the race, one from the point of view of each of the two characters involved.

a ....

b

UNIT 7 Time and history

In this unit you will look at more prefixes and the positioning of 'only'; think about dashes and sentence structures; and practise using pronouns of amount. You will write news headlines and read a timetable.

1 **Read the sentences below.**

  a Tick the sentences which are grammatically correct complete sentences.

  i That all depends.

  ii Although it was two o'clock in the morning, and everybody had been fast asleep for several hours.

  iii History shows that the same things happen time and time again, regardless.

  iv Would that she had never clapped eyes on them.

  v A most magnificent sight – one to remember for a lifetime.

  b Write as complete sentences the ones you have not ticked.

  ....

  ....

  ....

  ....

2 **Put either a single dash or a pair of dashes in the following speeches, to show either an additional thought or clarification (as in the last sentence in exercise 1a), or to create a parenthesis.**

  a Do you remember the time I suppose it must have been about 20 years ago when we first saw the Great Wall of China?

b I've been waiting for ages, thinking you weren't going to show up as I usually do.

c We aren't going to make it to the cinema in time and I hate missing the beginning of a film.

d If you don't think you will be able to wake up early enough, then you had better set an alarm or maybe even two alarms to be on the safe side.

e Haven't I told you a hundred times make that a million times not to come into the house wearing muddy shoes?

3 Give as many possible prefixes as you can think of to the following word stems.

a pose..

b spect..

c cover..

d vade..

e act..

f tract...

g serve..

h sist..

i mit...

UNIT 7 Time and history

4 For the following prefixes give:
- their meaning
- their opposite
- at least one example of a word beginning with each prefix.

Prefix	Meaning	Opposite	Example
a inter			
b pro			
c post			
d ex			
e hyper			

5 Make up headlines, of no more than six words, for the following news stories.

a A dangerous prisoner has escaped from jail and nobody knows how he succeeded in doing so.

....

b A woman found wandering in the woods has lost her memory and doesn't know who she is.

....

c A large sum of money has been won in a lottery but the winner cannot be traced.

....

d An art gallery has been robbed but the thieves took only a fake painting.

....

e There has been a reported sighting of an enormous cloud of locusts heading inland.

....

6 Put 'some', 'any', 'no' or 'none' in the gaps below.

a We don't have .... pears but we do have .... apples; there was .... delivery of fruit today. We've had .... since yesterday.

b .... body has been here since we left, although there is .... body here now, and I can't imagine why .... body should want to come here.

c Is there .... reason why you shouldn't arrange .... music lessons during the week when there are .... exams at school?

d There is .... doubt that if .... one can do it, she can, even though she's had .... health problems recently.

e They say that .... thing is better than .... thing, and that half a loaf is better than .... , but I don't agree with that .... more.

7 Rewrite the following sentences, inserting 'only' in the right place for the intended meaning. There is more than one possibility in some sentences.

a Be quick getting the coffees! There are a few minutes left before the bus leaves.

....

....

UNIT 7 Time and history

b If I had allowed a bit more time for the journey, I wouldn't have missed the plane that day.

c There were five at the beginning of the day, but by the end there were two.

d The person who understands how to do it isn't here at the moment. Can you come back later?

e They saw him; they didn't speak to him.

f They saw him; they didn't see her.

g They saw him; we didn't see him.

h He can teach English. He is not qualified to teach French.

i The museum allows viewing. Taking photographs or touching the exhibits is forbidden.

8 The timetable below is for the main railway line across Pakistan, and the route of Pakistan's most famous train, the Khyber Mail. There are lots of trains, but only the most important ones are shown here. All trains shown have a restaurant car.

	Karachi ➤ Lahore ➤ Peshawar							
Train No.:	27	41	7	15	1	107	101	103
Classes:	P,L,E	P,L,E	A,1,L,E	A,L,E	A,1,E	P,L,E	P,L,E	P,L,E
Karachi (Cantonment) depart	07:00 day 1	16:00 day 1	17:00 day 1	18:00 day 1	22:00 day 1	–	–	–
Hyderabad arr/dep	09:45 day 1	18:40 day 1	19:45 day 1	20:35 day 1	00:50 day 2	–	–	–
Rohri arr/dep	14:50 day 1	23:20 day 1	00:40 day 2	01:05 day 2	05:40 day 2	–	–	–
Multan (Cantonment) arr/dep	|	|	07:20 day 2	|	14:03 day 2	–	–	–
Lahore (Junction) arr/dep	02:45 day 2	10:15 day 2	14:15 day 2	12:00 day 2	21:40 day 2	07:00	07:30	16:30
Rawalpindi arr/dep	–	–	19:30 day 2	–	03:10 day 3	11:00	12:30	21:30
Attock arr/dep	–	–	–	–	04:30 day 3	–	–	–
Peshawar (City) arrive	–	–	–	–	06:20 day 3	–	–	–
Peshawar (Cantonment) arrive	–	–	–	–	06:40 day 3	–	–	–

A = air-conditioned sleeper, 1 = 1st class sleeper, L = air-conditioned lower class, P = Parlour car, E = Economy class

From A beginner's guide to train travel in Pakistan, *www.seat61.com*

UNIT 7 Time and history

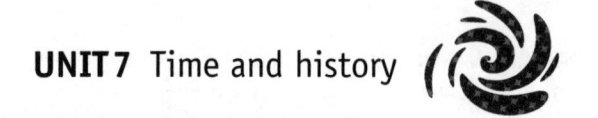

Write an email to a friend who is coming to visit you in Rawalpindi from Hyderabad and intends to travel by train in Economy class. Tell him or her the possible train numbers and departure times, how long the journey will take and the facilities available.

Dear ……………………………

UNIT 8 Exotic places

In this unit you will write imaginative and factual descriptions, sequencing ideas and using imagery. You will also practise forming complex sentences; and use colons and semi-colons, a variety of speech introduction words and similes and metaphors.

1 Write one-sentence speeches introduced by the following metaphorical words of animal sounds and give them appropriate speakers. For example:

bellowed → *The frustrated shop assistant suddenly bellowed, 'I really wish you'd make up your mind.'*

a squealed

....

....

b hissed

....

....

c snarled

....

....

d roared

....

....

e screeched

....

....

UNIT 8 Exotic places

2 **Read the passage below.**

a Put colons in the passage to show how they are used to introduce a list.

b Put semi-colons in the passage to show how they are used to separate items in a list.

> Those old days and all those far-off things have been locked away for so long that I thought they were gone forever the lions padding around outside my father's house the eagles circling over the mountain tops the bright African sun glinting on our spears and muskets and on the enemy's helmets and rifles.
>
> I was seven years old then. I didn't know anything about the world beyond our Abyssinian mountains. The sounds I heard were caused by a mixture of animal and human the whoop of hyenas at night the chanting of priests in the stillness of dawn the trample of horses' hooves the shouts of men the crackle of musket fire the clatter of spears the croaking of vultures. There were so many familiar smells the smoke of our fires the spices of our rich cooking the incense that scented my mother's house my father's sweat when he picked me up and I buried my face in his chest.
>
> *Adapted from* The Prince who Walked with Lions *by Elizabeth Laird*

3 Rewrite the second paragraph of the passage above using longer or complex sentences (i.e. without using the words 'but', 'and', 'or' or 'so'). Use present participles and a range of connectives to join the ideas together. You can reorder the material, make grammatical changes and insert extra words as necessary.

....

....

....

....

....

4 Read the passage below about the African island of Mauritius.

Mauritius . . .

is situated in the Indian Ocean, east of Africa

is a mountainous island

was captured by the British in 1810

grows sugarcane as its main crop

has a capital called Port Louis

was first explored by the Portuguese in 1505

became independent of the Dutch, French and British in 1968

is almost entirely surrounded by coral reefs

was the only native home of the dodo, before it became extinct in the 17th century

was known to Arab and Malay sailors as early as the 10th century

is a popular tourist destination, particularly for water sports enthusiasts

covers about 1865 square kilometres, with 330 km of coastline

has Hindu as its main religion

has four languages: Creole, Bhojpuri, French and English

has a population of 1.2 million and is the most densely populated African country

UNIT 8 Exotic places

a Reorder the 15 facts in the box in a logical sequence by putting a number next to each.

b Then think of ways to connect several facts in the same sentence, using a variety of methods.

c Write a description of Mauritius below, using approximately five sentences.

Cambridge Checkpoint English 8

5 **Imagine that you are walking through a tropical jungle.**

a Make notes of your perceptions under the headings of the five senses in the table below.

sight	
sound	
smell	
touch	
taste	

b Describe your experience using your notes above.

....

....

....

....

....

....

....

....

....

....

UNIT 8 Exotic places

6 **Look closely at the picture below.**

a Make notes of the features of the object.

....

....

....

....

....

....

....

....

....

....

....

b Think of similes and metaphors to help you describe the object and the actions depicted on it.

....

....

....

....

....

....

c Write a description of the object using evocative vocabulary and imagery.

UNIT 9 Travel and transport

This unit will give you practice in using adjectives and intensifiers to create descriptive language to evoke connotations.

1 Put an adverb and an adjective in front of each of the following nouns (e.g. *palace* → *sumptuously ornate palace*).

a villa ....

b lake ....

c castle ....

d mountain ....

e valley ....

f wall ....

g waterfall ....

h tower ....

i forest ....

j beach ....

Cambridge Checkpoint English 8

2 **Fill the ten gaps in the passage below with two possible words each:**

a to describe a thriving town

b to describe a run-down town.

> We arrived at our destination mid-morning and got off the bus. The first thing which struck us was how [1] .... the streets of the town were with shops which were [2] .... The people we saw all seemed to be [3] ...., and they were dressed [4] .... The buildings in the town centre looked [5] ...., having obviously been [6] .... The vehicles which passed us were [7] .... The music we could hear could be described as [8] .... All together the atmosphere was [9] .... and we found the town very [10] ....

a a thriving town

1 ....
2 ....
3 ....
4 ....
5 ....
6 ....
7 ....
8 ....
9 ....
10 ....

b a run-down town

1 ....
2 ....
3 ....
4 ....
5 ....
6 ....
7 ....
8 ....
9 ....
10 ....

UNIT 9 Travel and transport

3 Think of phrases consisting of an adverb, adjective and noun that you would use to create five different atmospheres and settings, e.g. *piercingly chill wind*.

a a very cold place

....

....

....

....

b a very hot place

....

....

....

....

c a very empty place

....

....

....

....

d a very crowded place

....

....

e a very frightening place

4 **Put appropriate and different intensifiers (e.g. *completely*, *very*) in the gaps in the following sentences.**

  a The view from the top of the mountain was .... amazing.

  b I have never seen anyone do anything quite .... dangerous.

  c He has .... this minute arrived.

  d The .... idea of it makes me feel .... ill.

  e You can tell that he is .... impressed by the way that he keeps looking in that .... direction.

5 **For each of the places below, write words or phrases to describe the connotations and the associations they have for you.**

  a dental surgery

UNIT 9 Travel and transport

b swimming pool

....

....

....

....

c campsite

....

....

....

....

d circus

....

....

....

....

....

e airport

....

....

....

....

6 Imagine that you wish to sell a means of transport that you own, e.g. a bicycle or skateboard. Write a one-paragraph advertisement for the item that makes it seem a desirable purchase.

FOR SALE

....

....

....

....

....

....

....

....

....

7 Underline in the passage below the phrases that are evocative. Then answer the questions that follow.

As she clung on to the ship's railings, bracing her body against the buffeting wind which was taking her breath away, she could feel the mounting waves swell and roll in a sickening see-saw rhythm. Chairs began to slide purposefully around the deck, as if mobilised and sent into enemy action. It was as if the ship was being grabbed and pulled sideways by a giant hand. The horizon was no longer horizontal, but tipped and lurched at acute angles, so that the sky and sea seemed to be battling for supremacy. The black bowl of cloud overhead, which had loomed

UNIT 9 Travel and transport

> out of nowhere and now threatened to pour out its contents to swamp the tiny humans beneath, was in league with the wrathful wind. It was clear that the tempestuous elements would show no mercy on the vulnerable vessel and its human cargo.

a What atmosphere has been created?

....

....

....

b Which descriptive devices are used?

....

....

....

c What are the recurring images?

....

....

....

d Which particularly powerful individual words are used?

....

....

....

e What connotations do they have?

....

....

....

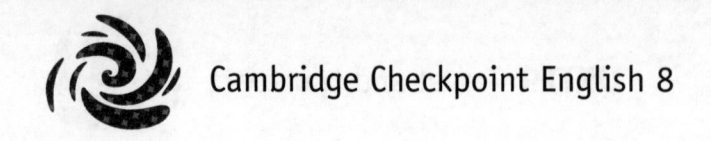

8 **Write your own description of a garden.**

Try to create a powerful atmosphere. Cover as many senses as possible, think about using a sustained image, and use evocative, unusual, polysyllabic words with interesting sounds.

....

....

....

....

....

....

....

....

....

....

....

....

....

....

....

....

....

....

....

....

....

UNIT 10 Animal behaviour

This unit gives you practice in vocabulary-building and evaluating synonyms. You will also practise paraphrasing; using emphatic adverbials; and selecting, sequencing and connecting material.

1 Read the passage, which is the focus of the questions in this unit.

There are two types of elephant: African and Asian (or Indian). They are the largest living terrestrial mammal. African elephants are larger than Asian elephants, over 3 metres tall and weighing more than 6 tonnes. Despite its weight, an elephant can walk silently because of the thick padding covering the sole of its foot. **As a rule**, females are smaller than males. Both species of elephant can live to be 70 years old.

Elephants live in dense forest and open plains, and **their diet is herbivorous**. Their muscular trunk has many purposes: nose, hand, signalling device, tool, water siphon and weapon, among others. This unique physical feature can perform delicate movements of picking berries and stroking, as well as tearing down trees or fighting. Elephants are capable of showing recognition and affection, which they do to other elephants they meet at watering-holes by entwining their trunks. The difference in trunk between the two types is that the African elephant has two finger-like structures at its tip and the Asian has only one. Asian elephants have light grey/brown skin, whereas African elephants are darker coloured.

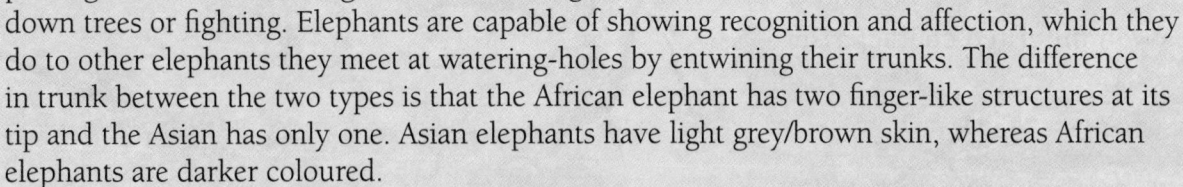

Their other remarkable feature is their tusks, an indicator of age. A third of the tusk grows inside their skull. Over the years poachers have killed the animals with the largest tusks, so huge sizes of tusk are no longer found on elephants in Africa, as tusk size is **an inherited characteristic**. Female African elephants have tusks, but only males have them in the Asian species. Tusks differ in shape and direction and are a means of identifying individual elephants.

The large oblong teeth of elephants have ridges. When the last one wears down, the elephant can no longer chew food and **dies of malnutrition**. Elephants need a huge amount of vegetation and spend 16 hours a day eating. They also need approximately 900 litres of daily drinking water. Asian elephants have a more varied diet, as they have access to bamboo and fruits such as mango.

Cambridge Checkpoint English 8

> African elephants' ears are twice as large as those of Asian elephants and are a different shape, similar to a map of Africa. Elephants use their ears to signal; when alarmed or angry they spread them and bring them forward. They can also signal over many kilometres by calling. Their body temperature is controlled by losing heat through flapping their ears.
>
> Elephants form family groups and **the herd is presided over** by the females; adult males tend to live a solitary existence. Mature females usually give birth to only one calf at a time. Elephants are known to be highly intelligent, with good recall and complex social structures. It is a myth that there are secret elephant burial grounds to which the bones of dead elephants are taken by the living ones. It is true, however, that they take care of weak and injured members and appear to grieve over a dead companion.
>
> It is a sad fact that their only predators are human. Owing to overhunting and the spread of the desert, the African elephant population is in decline, and it has already disappeared from North Africa, where they were common in Roman times. Increasing human settlement has displaced elephant habitats and restricted their movements. Many now live in controlled areas. Asian elephants also suffer from shrinking habitats and loss of traditional migration routes.

2 Rewrite the phrases in bold in the passage using your own words.

a As a rule

....

b their diet is herbivorous

....

c an inherited characteristic

....

d dies of malnutrition

....

e the herd is presided over by

....

UNIT 10 Animal behaviour

3 For each of the words from the passage listed below, we have provided three possible synonyms (words with a similar meaning). Put a number 1 to 3 above the words to show increasing order of their strength of meaning.

a **solitary**: lone, lonely, single

b **complex**: complicated, confused, intricate

c **secret**: covered, hidden, mysterious

d **controlled**: restricted, supervised, forbidden

e **common**: ordinary, frequent, widespread

4 Think of related words, containing the same stem, for the following words from the passage.

a terrestrial

....

b type

....

c indicator

....

d solitary

....

e signal

....

5 Give antonyms (words with an opposite meaning) for the following words from the passage.

a dense ....

b delicate ....

c approximately ....

d varied ....

e decline ....

6 **Write true or false next to the following statements about elephants.**

a African and Asian elephants can live equally long. ....

b African and Asian elephants have identical diets. ....

c Elephants die when they can no longer chew food. ....

d Elephant family groups are dominated by the males. ....

e There are secret elephant burial grounds. ....

UNIT 10 Animal behaviour

7 Divide the facts in the passage into two columns.

African elephants	Asian elephants
....	....
....	....
....	....
....	....
....	....
....	....
....	....
....	....
....	....

8 Answer the questions below.

  a Consider these alternative titles for the passage and tick the one you think would be best.

  Elephants ☐

  The behaviour of elephants ☐

  African versus Asian elephants ☐

  b Explain in one sentence why you think that the title you chose is the best of the three for the passage.

  ....

  ....

  ....

Cambridge Checkpoint English 8

c Can you think of an even more suitable title for the passage, and explain why?

....

....

....

9 Read through the passage again.

a Put brackets round any information in the passage that you do not think is essential for an encyclopedia entry for elephants.

b Group the remaining information under topic headings (e.g. trunk) and decide on the most logical order in which to sequence it.

c Write a new and more concise version of the passage below, under your chosen title, connecting the facts you have numbered in exercise 9b into longer and more complex sentences.

....

....

....

....

....

....

....

....

....

....

UNIT 10 Animal behaviour

10 Now look at the passage again, and underline material to use for a talk on elephants to be given to primary age children. You will probably want to include facts which you deleted from your summary in exercise 9 to make the talk more interesting. You will also need to make the style more appropriate for the new audience by:

- adding emphatic adverbials
- simplifying the vocabulary
- using shorter sentences.

Elephants are surprising creatures

11 Collect notes below, in two columns, for a debate on whether elephants should be used in circuses. You can develop ideas from the passage, and also add ideas of your own.

FOR	AGAINST

UNIT 11 Music and dance

This unit focuses on figurative language, and negative phrasing and understatement for emphasis. It gives you practice in tense usage with time adverbs and adverbial phrases and the passive form; using colloquial and idiomatic English; and using 'continual' and 'continuously'. You will also revise hyphens and commas.

1 **Explain the following cliché images in non-figurative language.**

   a The row was just a storm in a tea-cup.

   ....

   ....

   b She looked like a cat that has got the cream.

   ....

   ....

   c His mind went blank at the start of the exam.

   ....

   d The nervous musician was all fingers and thumbs.

   ....

   e The audience brought the house down at the end of the show.

   ....

2 **Think of images to express the following ideas and emotions (e.g. *she was boiling over with enthusiasm*).**

   a excitement

   ....

   b energy

   ....

c anger

....

d happiness

....

e strength

....

3 **Explain the effect of the use of the following phrases.**

a He said not a word (compared with *He didn't speak*).

....

b She wasn't exactly surprised when he arrived (compared with *She was unsurprised when he arrived*).

....

c I went there rarely (compared with *I didn't go there often*).

....

d It was no longer considered unacceptable (compared with *It was considered acceptable now*).

....

e There was no possibility of his agreeing to the proposal (compared with *It was impossible that he would agree to the proposal*).

....

4 **Paraphrase the following uses of understatement, the opposite of hyperbole.**

a I will not give you a penny more.

....

UNIT 11 Music and dance

b It takes a week or two to become the world's greatest ballerina.

....

....

c He thought that the police raid on his apartment might mean that he was in slight trouble.

....

....

d He overreacted just a little by cancelling the entire performance.

....

....

e It is not usually a good idea to jump out of a plane without a parachute.

....

....

5 **Circle where words should be hyphenated in the following passage.**

The musical was staged in the local theatre the day before yesterday. The amateur and under experienced dancers put on a good performance. The make up of the group was a wide range of ages and abilities, and included both teenage girls and middle aged women, as well as twenty something males. The red haired principal dancer was a knock out in the role of the sweet tempered princess with the evil half sister and jealous brother in law. The costumes, mostly pale coloured and silver striped, were designed by a recently retired ex model. The well disposed audience, consisting of not so experienced ballet spectators, was highly appreciative of the year long effort to produce the show.

Cambridge Checkpoint English 8

6 Write the correct time adverbs in the passage below.

It was many years .... when I first heard Luciano Pavarotti, the opera star, perform in Italy. .... that time he was .... quite famous, and .... the following year he had become a household name. I bought every one of his recordings .... the next decade, ... 1990 and 2000, including .... the time I was living in China, ... 1994 .... 1996. .... then I haven't listened to him ...., though I .... possess those CDs.

7 Put a tick above the commas that are being used correctly, and a cross when they are not, in the following dialogue.

'Hi, Angela. Do you fancy going to a concert, tomorrow?'

'Well, Dean, it depends what it is, obviously.'

'You know that band, which has been on the radio recently? The one with a name, beginning with W.'

'You mean, the Wandering Wombats? Or are you referring to Wild West? I like the second of those, but I hate the first. They sound like, the kind of music my grandparents listen to.'

'Oh dear, I'm not sure now, which it is. Can I get back to you, later?'

UNIT 11 Music and dance

8 Decide whether the active or passive form is more appropriate in the following pairs of sentences, tick your choice, and then explain the reason for it.

a Breakfast is served from six a.m. onwards.
   We serve breakfast from six a.m. onwards.

   ....

b We enjoyed the singing and dancing.
   The singing and dancing was enjoyed by us.

   ....

c Let it be known that the time has come.
   Let people know that the time has come.

   ....

d The experiment must be supervised at all times.
   Someone must supervise the experiment at all times.

   ....

e You have achieved the impossible!
   The impossible has been achieved by you!

   ....

9 Change the colloquial and idiomatic expressions below into formal English.

a It's not down to me.

   ....

b I'm not carrying the can for this shambles.

   ....

c Don't shoot the messenger.

   ....

d You need to chill.

....

e I'm not going to take it lying down.

....

10 Which of the following should not be written as one word? Write them as they should be split.

a nevertheless	....	**f** aswellas	....
b infact	....	**g** infrontof	....
c notwithstanding	....	**h** hereby	....
d nowadays	....	**i** ourselves	....
e inspiteof	....	**j** percent	....

11 Put 'continual(ly)' or 'continuous(ly)' in the gaps in the sentences below.

a The rain was .... , making it impossible to leave the house.

b You .... tell me that you don't like sport, so why have you decided to try out for the football team?

UNIT 11 Music and dance

c If something happens non-stop, then we use the word .... ,
but if it happens with pauses in between, then the right word is ....

d This has been a .... problem for the last year, so I shall have to buy a new computer.

e To become a good musician or dancer, you have to practise ....

UNIT 12 A load of nonsense

In this unit you look at some homographs and pronunciation and spelling anomalies. It also gives you practice in using commas in defining and non-defining relative clauses, writing reported speech and forms of the future tense. You also look at colons, semi-colons and other punctuation, and you write a description of a process and a place.

1 **Homographs are words that are spelt the same but have different meanings and may have different pronunciations.**

  a Write two sentences for each of these homographs to show two meanings of the word (some have more than two).

  i race

  ....

  ....

  ii bow

  ....

  ....

  iii sole

  ....

  ....

  iv ring

  ....

  ....

  v tip

  ....

  ....

UNIT 12 A load of nonsense

vi rose

....

....

vii wind

....

....

viii mean

....

....

ix row

....

....

x light

....

....

b List all the other homographs you can think of.

....

....

....

....

....

Cambridge Checkpoint English 8

2 Circle the words below which are the odd ones out in terms of pronunciation.

  a bow   row   mow

  b vow   low   now

  c mood   blood   food

  d read   lead   bead

  e dough   plough   bough

3 Decide which of these words are spelt correctly. Circle each word which is not spelt correctly, and give the correct spelling below it.

  a wrestle   wrist   wrong   wring   wrattle

  ....

  b gnaw   gnarled   gnatter   gnome   gnat

  ....

  c knestle   knot   knit   knee   knack

  ....

  d ghastly   ghetto   ghist   gherkin   ghost

  ....

  e rhubarb   rhyme   rhythm   rhandom   rheumatism

  ....

4 Put a comma where necessary in the following sentences, depending on whether they contain a defining or non-defining relative clause.

  a Balloons appeal to children who like bright colours.

  b Children who like nonsense also like magic.

  c The word which comes to mind is 'crazy'!

UNIT 12 A load of nonsense

d If the person whom you are looking for isn't available the receptionist who is always at the front desk will take a message.

e I don't know which is worse: the student who is always late or the student who never does any homework.

5 Complete the five sentences below using the different ways of forming the future tense, according to how soon and how definitely the event will happen.

a He will see ....

b He is to see ....

c He is going to see ....

d He is about to see ....

e He is seeing ....

6 Put at least one of each of the following punctuation marks in the following passage.

full stop   comma   dash   hyphen   colon   semi-colon   apostrophe

Zorbing

Zorbing is one of the latest extreme sports it makes you feel as though you are travelling in a hamsters exercise ball you can do it over land or water it may seem mad but it is surprisingly popular in New Zealand and elsewhere just remaining upright is a great achievement basically you hurtle down a hill in nothing more than an inflatable ball as protection the inner capsule suspended on nylon strings protects you from the bumps on your head over heels ride.

7 Put colons and semi-colons in the correct places in each of the sentences below.

  a There were many things I had to remember to pack for the bike trip antimalaria tablets sticking plasters in case of accidents sunscreen and a sunhat waterproof clothing plenty of water.

  b He would always remember the Scout motto 'Be prepared' it had not changed since 1910.

  c This is a famous quotation by Julius Caesar I came I saw I conquered.

  d Many times the wolf approached the edge of the farm many times it hid in fear it was the primeval fear of humans.

  e There are many kinds of nonsense verse poems with made up or silly words in poems which are about things which cannot happen or are illogical poems which don't make sense at all.

8 Read the following passage and then answer the questions.

Not always was the Kangaroo as now we do behold him, but a Different Animal with four short legs. He was grey and he was woolly, and his pride was inordinate: he danced on an outcrop in the middle of Australia, and he went to the Little God Nqa.

He went to Nqa at six before breakfast, saying make me different from all other animals by five this afternoon.

Up jumped Nqa from his seat on the sandflat and shouted go away!

He was grey and he was woolly, and his pride was inordinate: he danced on a rock-ledge in the middle of Australia, and he went to the Middle God Nquing.

UNIT 12 A load of nonsense

> He went to Nquing at eight after breakfast, saying make me different from all other animals; make me, also, wonderfully popular by five this afternoon.
>
> Up jumped Nquing from his burrow in the spinifex and shouted go away!
>
> He was grey and he was woolly, and his pride was inordinate: he danced on a sandbank in the middle of Australia, and he went to the Big God Nqong.
>
> He went to Nqong at ten before dinner-time, saying make me different from all other animals; make me popular and wonderfully run after by five this afternoon.
>
> Up jumped Nqong from his bath in the salt-pan and shouted yes, I will!
>
> *Adapted from* The Sing-Song of Old Man Kangaroo *by Rudyard Kipling*

a Put speech punctuation in the passage, including commas and capital letters to precede a speech, where required. Use double inverted commas around the speech.

b Rewrite as reported speech the parts of the passage containing speech.

Cambridge Checkpoint English 8

9 **Describe one of the following processes, in five stages.**

   a How to make scrambled eggs.

   b How to catch a fish.

   c How to upload a photograph to a social networking page.

   1 ....
   2 ....
   3 ....
   4 ....
   5 ....

10 Describe this building using the lines on the next page.

UNIT 12 A load of nonsense

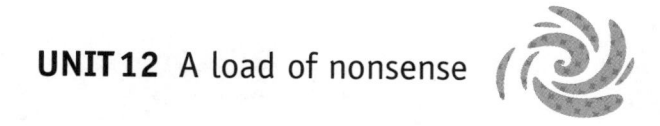

Acknowledgements

The authors and publishers acknowledge the following sources of copyright material and are grateful for the permissions granted. While every effort has been made, it has not always been possible to identify the sources of all the material used, or to trace all copyright holders. If any omissions are brought to our notice, we will be happy to include the appropriate acknowledgements on reprinting.

p. 14 'The story of how chess was invented' by Omar Syed from http://arimaa.com/arimaa/links/chessStory.html; p. 21 © Telegraph Media Group Limited 2002; p. 37 from *The Story of My Life* by Helen Keller, copyright © 1958 by Helen Keller, used by permission from The American Foundation for the Blind Helen Keller Archives, all rights reserved; p. 53 from *The Prince who Walked with Lions* by Elizabeth Laird, Macmillan Children's Books, 2012, adapted with permission of the publisher